In the Footsteps of Explorers

Samuel de Champlain

From New France to Cape Cod

Adrianna Morganelli

Crabtree Publishing Company

www.crabtreebooks.com

Crabtree Publishing Company

www.crabtreebooks.com

For my parents, Nick and Adele

Coordinating editor: Ellen Rodger
Series editor: Carrie Gleason
Editors: Rachel Eagen, L. Michelle Nielsen
Design and production coordinator: Rosie Gowsell
Cover design and production assistance: Samara Parent
Art direction: Rob MacGregor
Scanning technician: Arlene Arch-Wilson
Photo research: Allison Napier

Consultants: Stacy Hasselbacher, Tracey Neikirk, The Mariners' Museum, Newport News, Virginia

Photo Credits: British Museum, London, UK/Bridgeman Art Library: pp. 16-17; Peabody Essex Museum, Salem, Massachusetts, USA/Bridgeman Art Library: p. 25 (top); Private Collection, Archives Charmet/Bridgeman Art Library: cover, p. 11; Private Collection, The Stapleton Collection/Bridgeman Art Library: pp. 14-15; Archivo Iconografico, S.A./Corbis: p.14; Nathan Benn/Corbis: p. 27; Bettmann/Corbis: pp. 8-9, p. 12, p. 21; Robert Holmes/Corbis: p. 7

(bottom); Christopher J. Morris/Corbis: p. 31; Lee Snider/Photo Images/Corbis: p. 30; The Granger Collection: p. 23; Hsianyo Kuo/istock International: p. 5 (middle); North Wind Picture Archive: p. 6 (bottom), pp. 12-13, p. 18, p. 19, p. 20, p. 22, pp. 24-25, p. 26, p. 28, p. 29 (both); Public Domain, Credit: C. W. Jefferys: p. 25 (bottom). Other images from stock cd

Illustrations: Lauren Fast: p. 4

Cartography: Jim Chernishenko: title page, p. 10

Cover: An illustration of Champlain sailing up the St. Lawrence River on his 1603 voyage.

Title page: Samuel de Champlain was a French explorer who is known as the "Father of New France" for his journeys through present-day Quebec, Canada.

Sidebar icon: Animals such as beavers were hunted for their furs.

Crabtree Publishing Company

www.crabtreebooks.com   1-800-387-7650

Cataloging-in-Publication Data
Morganelli, Adrianna, 1979-
  Samuel de Champlain : from New France to Cape Cod / written by Adrianna Morganelli.
   p. cm. -- (In the footsteps of explorers)
  Includes index.
  ISBN-13: 978-0-7787-2414-8 (rlb)
  ISBN-10: 0-7787-2414-X (rlb)
  ISBN-13: 978-0-7787-2450-6 (pb)
  ISBN-10: 0-7787-2450-6 (pb)
 1. Champlain, Samuel de, 1567-1635--Juvenile literature. 2. Explorers--America--Biography--Juvenile literature. 3. Explorers--France--Biography--Juvenile literature. 4. New France--Discovery and exploration--Juvenile literature. 5. America--Discovery and exploration--French--Juvenile literature. I. Title. II. Series.

 F1030.1.M67 2005
 910'.92--dc22

                                   2005014863
                                       LC

**Published in
the United States**
PMB 16A
350 Fifth Ave.
Suite 3308
New York, NY
10118

**Published
in Canada**
616 Welland Ave.
St. Catharines
Ontario, Canada
L2M 5V6

**Published in the
United Kingdom**
73 Lime Walk
Headington
Oxford
OX3 7AD
United Kingdom

**Published
in Australia**
386 Mt. Alexander Rd.
Ascot Vale (Melbourne)
VIC 3032

Contents

Father of New France

Samuel de Champlain was a French explorer who made many voyages from France to North America in search of a trade route to Asia, and of land for settlers. Champlain explored North America, founded a colony in present-day Canada, and became known as the "Father of New France."

Land of Opportunity

Champlain embarked on 21 voyages across the Atlantic to North America to map the land and find a suitable site for a French fur-trading colony. He befriended the Huron, as well as Algonquian-speaking peoples and waged war against their enemy, the **Haudenosaunee**, or Iroquois. Champlain established thriving **settlements** in Canada that contributed to the growing wealth of New France. New France, a French colony, grew and eventually included southeast Canada, the Great Lakes region, and the Mississippi Valley.

Life in France

The early life of Samuel de Champlain was not well documented. Most historians believe that he was born in 1567. As a boy, he lived in the seaport town of Brouage, France, with his mother Marguerite Le Roy, and his father Antoine Champlain, who was a sea captain. Unlike other children of Brouage, Champlain could read and write. Historians believe that he received training in **navigation**, drawing, and mapmaking at home. As a young man, he joined in a war for control of Brouage. Champlain served in the French army from 1594 to 1598.

(above) Samuel de Champlain explored North America and established a settlement at Quebec City.

Champlain's Reports

In 1603, Champlain explored the land along the St. Lawrence River in search of a site to erect a French settlement. In a report of his findings to the king of France, Champlain wrote of the benefits of present-day Montreal, Quebec as a potential site.

"As for the country itself, it is beautiful and agreeable, and it brings all sorts of grain and seed to maturity. There are in it all the varieties of trees we have in our forests on this side of the ocean and many fruits, although they are wild for lack of cultivation: such as butternut trees, cherry-trees, plum-trees, vines, raspberries, strawberries, gooseberries and red currants, and several other small fruits, which are quite good. There are also several sorts of useful herbs and roots. Fish are plentiful in the rivers, along which are meadows and game in vast quantity."

Champlain told his king about the many fruits that grew wild in North America.

- 1567 -
Samuel de Champlain born in Brouage, France.

- July 3, 1608 -
Champlain founds present-day Quebec City, in Canada.

- December 25, 1635 -
Champlain dies in Quebec City, Canada.

Trade and Exploration

The thirst for wealth from the spice trade, and the power wealth brought, led many European countries to send out ships of exploration in the 1500s and 1600s. These ships brought explorers to the New World, where they discovered new commodities to trade.

Europe's Desire for Wealth

During the **Middle Ages**, valuable spices and silks were brought to Europe from Asia via overland trade routes. **Arab** traders became wealthy by controlling these trade routes. Many European countries wanted to become wealthy themselves by finding a sea route to Asia so they could trade directly for spices and silk. They sent out ships of exploration to find the Moluccas, a chain of islands in present-day Indonesia, where some spices, such as cloves and nutmeg, grew. Explorers who sailed west from Europe ran into the lands of North, Central, and South America. Over time, Spain, Portugal, France, Holland, and England established trading posts and colonies in these new lands, which they called the New World. Settlers traded furs, fished, and mined for gold and silver.

(background) In 1497, John Cabot, an Italian who explored for England, announced that the Grand Banks along the coast of Newfoundland were teeming with codfish. Many Portuguese and Spanish fishers already knew the Grand Banks were one of the best fishing grounds in the world. Cabot's announcement brought even more European fishers to the New World.

France Takes Part

King Francois I of France was impressed with Spain's growing wealth from its empire in the Americas. He sent French explorers to claim land in the New World. The king believed that a passage to Asia lay north of Newfoundland and sent explorer Jacques Cartier on an expedition to find it in 1534. Cartier's attempt to establish a colony in the New World was unsuccessful and he failed to find riches or the route to Asia, called the Northwest Passage. The French continued to visit North America for its fish, timber, and furs. Many French fishers sailed to Canada's East Coast to fish for cod and trade tools and blankets for bear and beaver skins with the Native peoples.

Beaver Hats

During the 1500s, the French traded with the Native peoples of North America to feed a craze in Europe for fur hats. Native trappers were given knives, kettles, beads, and blankets in exchange for beaver pelts. Thousands of pelts were shipped to France every year from Tadoussac, France's first fur-trading post, in what is today the province of Quebec. In Europe, hat makers shaved the soft, fine hair of beaver pelts and crushed them together to form stylish felt hats. The European craze for these felt hats continued until the mid-1800s.

- 1492 -
Italian explorer Christopher Columbus sails across the Atlantic Ocean and reaches America, which he mistakes for Asia.

- 1497 -
John Cabot sails from England in search of the Northwest Passage to Asia and explores Canada's East Coast.

- 1534 -
French explorer Jacques Cartier sails up the St. Lawrence River and claims Quebec's Gaspe Peninsula for France.

Champlain's Early Life

On an early voyage to the New World, Champlain kept detailed journals. The journals included maps and illustrations and won him the favor of the King.

An Opportunity

Champlain's first recorded sailing voyage was from France to Spain with his uncle. They brought Spanish troops home to Spain after a war in Brouage. A Spanish admiral was impressed with the speed of the ship and hired it for a voyage to the Spanish colonies in the New World. Yearly visits were made there to supply the colonies with goods they needed in return for gold, silver, and dyes.

To the New World!

In January 1599, Champlain crossed the Atlantic Ocean to reach the Caribbean island of Guadeloupe. After sailing through the Virgin Islands, Champlain's ship anchored at the harbor of San Juan in Puerto Rico. There, Champlain took notes and sketched the tropical trees, plants, animals, and birds. Champlain's ship sailed on to Mexico, Panama, Cuba, and Colombia before returning to Spain in 1601.

Support from the French King

Champlain returned to France in 1603 and gave King Henry IV an illustrated book of his travels in the New World. King Henry was impressed and eager to learn more. He believed that if the French settled in the New World, wealth would be sent back to France. The king granted Champlain a small yearly income and a title of **nobility**. Champlain was sent back to the New World to search for a water route to Asia and a site for a fur-trading settlement.

(background) Champlain gained favor in the court of France's King Henry IV when the king learned through Champlain's journals that there were riches to be found in the New World.

Brave New World

Champlain set sail on his second voyage to the New World on March 15, 1603, with a fleet of three ships sponsored, or paid for, by the governor of Dieppe, France. The goal of the voyage was to find a suitable place for French colonists to settle.

A Promise

The ships weathered storms and crossed to the Grand Banks of Newfoundland. They entered the St. Lawrence River and anchored in the harbor of Tadoussac, a site near the mouth of the Saguenay River. Champlain came ashore and found a group of Montagnais people celebrating a victory over their enemies, the Iroquois. With the help of two Montagnais **interpreters**, the French brought greetings from the king and promised to help them defeat the Iroquois.

Future Prospects

Champlain sailed from Tadoussac along the Saguenay River. He saw Quebec while exploring the St. Lawrence River, and was impressed by the **fertile** land that was lush with grape vines and fruit trees. His Montagnais guides told him of a great sea to the west that never froze. Champlain believed the sea was the Pacific Ocean and that he was near the passage to Asia, but the Montagnais were referring to the Great Lakes.

St. Lawrence River

Habitation (Quebec)

Montreal

Port Royal

Cape Cod

Atlantic Ocean

North America

First Voyage:

Second Voyage:

(left) After his first voyage to New France, Champlain made 20 more trips across the Atlantic.

A New Expedition

Champlain and the fleet returned to Tadoussac, where the French traded with the Montagnais for beaver pelts and dried codfish for their return voyage across the Atlantic. When he returned to France, Champlain informed King Henry how the land along the St. Lawrence River was perfect for a French settlement, and that the river could be the route to Asia. A wealthy friend of the king, Pierre du Gua, Sieur de Monts, offered to sponsor a voyage to the New World to establish a French colony in exchange for a ten-year **monopoly** of the fur trade in New France. King Henry IV granted Champlain permission to join de Monts' expedition to make reports and maps. Champlain and the crew were also ordered to make peace with the Native peoples who lived there, **convert** them to **Christianity**, and search for gold and silver deposits that they could mine.

(background) *Champlain traveled the Lachine Rapids, near present-day Montreal, in small birchbark canoes made by Native peoples. The French ships were too large and not suited to the rivers.*

Founding of Acadia

Champlain helped establish French settlements in Acadia. Acadia was a territory between the St. Lawrence River and the Atlantic Ocean that included present-day Nova Scotia, New Brunswick, Prince Edward Island, Cape Breton Island, and eastern Maine.

The Grand Expedition

Champlain sailed from France for the New World with a fleet much larger than that of his last expedition. Two ships carried 120 colonists, including carpenters, laborers, **stonemasons,** and soldiers to guard against attack. Surgeons were onboard to care for the colonists' health, as well as a **Roman Catholic** priest to say **mass,** hear **confessions** and convert the Native peoples of the land to Christianity. Two fur-trading ships and a whaling ship also joined the expedition.

(below) The French brought priests to preach to the Native peoples who lived near French settlements.

> (background) *The expedition settled on the island of Ste. Croix, in New Brunswick. After a terrible winter, they abandoned their settlement and built a new settlement at Port Royal.*

The Search is On

The fleet planned to sail up the St. Lawrence River, but while crossing the Atlantic Ocean, de Monts decided to search for a site to build a settlement on the Atlantic Coast. A monopoly over the fur trade depended on de Monts establishing a permanent French settlement in the New World, and he was determined to do so. Champlain explored the coast of Nova Scotia and the Bay of Fundy, where he discovered a natural harbor, known today as the Annapolis Basin. Champlain estimated the basin could hold at least 2,000 ships and felt the colonists should settle at a site on the north shore of the harbor that he named Port Royal. Unsure about the site, de Monts decided they should continue looking along the coast of New Brunswick.

Ste. Croix

The fleet entered the mouth of the Ste. Croix River, located on the present-day border of the United States and Canada. De Monts chose Ste. Croix Island, in present-day Maine, as a suitable site to build the French settlement. The colonists worked through the summer to build a **barricade** that surrounded a cannon so they could defend against attack from sea. They also cleared trees on the island to build houses, a storehouse, kitchen, chapel, **forge**, and hand mill to grind grain. Fields were cleared along the riverbanks and planted with **rye**, and every colonist had his own garden.

- March 7, 1604 -

Champlain sails from France to set up a settlement in Acadia.

- 1604 -

A settlement is built on Ste. Croix Island.

- 1605 -

The Port Royal settlement is established.

- September 3, 1607 -

Champlain sails from Acadia for France.

Fate of Ste. Croix

The colonists soon regreted settling on Ste. Croix Island. There was little fresh water available and the sandy soil of the island did not support vegetables or crops. During the winter, the island was unprotected from the harsh northwest winds. The men ate frozen salted meat and vegetables and drank melted snow. Many colonists suffered from scurvy, a disease caused by lack of vitamin C found in fresh fruit and vegetables. Thirty-five of the 79 colonists died during the winter at Ste. Croix. The remaining settlers decided to abandon Ste. Croix and look for a new site.

Colony at Port Royal

Champlain set sail to search for a new place to build a settlement. De Monts decided they should return to Port Royal. This time, the colonists learned from their mistakes. They constructed a settlement with buildings located very close to each other to conserve heat. The colonists also built a large storehouse for grain and other supplies. Port Royal was occupied until 1607, when the French king ended de Monts' fur trade monopoly. The settlement could not survive without the money from the fur trade. Champlain, de Monts, and the colonists left for France. Champlain returned the next year, this time to establish a permanent fur trading post on the St. Lawrence River.

(top) In 1867, a boy named Edward Lee found what is thought to be Champlain's astrolabe in Ontario, Canada. An astrolabe is a navigational instrument.

(background) In June 1605, the settlement at Ste. Croix was abandoned. Champlain explored and mapped the East Coast harbors of Maine, Boston, Plymouth, and Cape Cod, looking for a new site for a settlement.

Colonizing New France

Champlain returned to New France in 1608, and set up a settlement, which he called Habitation, along the St. Lawrence River. Habitation nearly failed in its first year as settlers were weakened by a brutal winter and lack of food.

The Quebec Habitation

The second attempt to establish a French settlement in the New World nearly ended in disaster. At Habitation, colonists constructed houses and storehouses that were **fortified** with **ramparts** and moats, and land was cleared for farms and gardens. During their first harsh winter, many colonists suffered from scurvy and **dysentery**. Only eight of the 24 colonists survived.

Protecting the Fur Trade

Champlain wanted to build French settlements throughout Canada. During his first winter at Habitation, he befriended the Montagnais and learned more about the battles they fought against their enemy, the Iroquois. He formed an **alliance** with two groups of Algonquian-speaking peoples, the Montagnais and the Algonquin, as well as the Huron peoples to ensure the success of future French fur-trading settlements in their lands.

(background) On their way to battle with the Iroquois, Champlain and the Native peoples paddled up the Richelieu River and sailed along a lake. He named the lake, which is in present-day New York and Quebec, Lake Champlain.

- July 3, 1608 -

Champlain founds Habitation in present-day Quebec City.

- July 30, 1609 -

Champlain's first battle with the Iroquois.

- Winter 1609 -

Champlain returns to France.

(background) When Champlain returned to New France in 1610, he again agreed to go to war with the enemies of the Huron and Algonquian, the Haudenosaunee, or Iroquois Confederacy. As they approached the Iroquois' log fortress, an arrow split the tip of Champlain's ear and pierced his neck. After a fierce battle, only 15 Iroquois survived.

The First Battle

In the spring of 1609, Champlain and three of his men set out in canoes with about 60 Huron and Algonquian. They headed toward Iroquois lands on the St. Lawrence River. While paddling near Ticonderoga, in present-day New York, they were sighted by a party of Mohawk, who were members of the Haudenosaunee, or Iroquois Confederacy. At dawn, the Huron and Algonquian went ashore to face the Iroquois. Both sides were ready to fight. When Champlain approached, the Iroquois readied their bows and arrows. Champlain fired his **arquebus** killing two Iroquois chiefs and wounding a third. The Iroquois were terrified of Champlain's weapon and fled into the forest. Champlain chased them and shot several more as they tried to escape.

Competition for the French

After the cancellation of de Monts' fur trade monopoly, traders from other European countries began claiming land along the St. Lawrence River. In 1611, Champlain returned to Quebec in search of another site for a fur-trading settlement. He chose the site of present-day Montreal, which he named Place Royale. The settlement was not built until after Champlain's death, and it later become the center of the colony's fur trade. The king gave Champlain the job of running New France in 1612.

(right) Native arrows were deadly but they were no match for French firearms.

Fighting the Iroquois

Champlain's early decision to fight with the Algonquian and Huron against the Iroquois meant that the French were almost continually at war with the Iroquois.

Deciding on War

The 1609 battle between the French and the Iroquois in what is now New York made the Iroquois hate the French. The victory also made Champlain think that the Iroquois would be easy to get rid of. Upon arriving in New France in 1615, Champlain and his Native allies were determined to wage another war against the Iroquois. A victory would secure the Huron as fur-trading partners and allow the French to explore the Iroquois' lands. Champlain followed the Ottawa River and mapped the shoreline of Lake Huron before reaching Huronia, what the French called Huron territory. Huron allies, the Carantouan, promised to send 500 warriors to help them fight the Iroquois.

(background) The Huron war with the Iroquois existed long before the Huron met and became allies with the French. It continued long after Champlain's death. The feud ended when the Iroquois finally defeated the Huron in 1650.

Angering the Allies

Champlain's men traveled through the Bay of Quinte on the north shore of Lake Ontario and crossed the lake where they spotted a fortified Iroquois village on Lake Onondaga, in present-day New York. From behind the walls of their fort, the Iroquois attacked Champlain's group with a shower of poisoned arrows. Many Huron were wounded, as well as Champlain, who was pierced twice in the leg. When the Huron's allies, the Carantouan, failed to arrive, Champlain knew his group was outnumbered and was forced to admit defeat. The Huron felt betrayed because Champlain had promised them victory over the Iroquois. They refused to provide Champlain with a canoe to return to Habitation, and insisted he return to Huronia to plan a future battle.

(right) Injured during battle with the Iroquois, Champlain was carried to safety on the back of a Huron ally.

- July 20, 1629 -

England takes possession of New France.

- May 29, 1632 -

The Treaty of Saint-Germain-en-Laye is signed, returning New France to French rule.

The English Threat

The fledgling settlement of Habitation depended on supplies from France for its survival. By 1628, the English were eyeing new territory in North America. They prevented French supply ships from docking, which nearly starved the setters of Habitation.

The Letter

In 1628, English captain David Kirk delivered a letter to Champlain demanding the surrender of Habitation. The letter explained that Kirk was sent from the King of England to take possession of New France. Champlain did not surrender, and the English blocked French ships from bringing food and supplies.

Misery and Surrender

The settlers **rationed** their dwindling food supply. The Montagnais traded dried eel with the French for beaver fur, and taught them how to find edible roots. The next summer, three English ships returned to Habitation to ask Champlain to surrender. He had no choice but to give up the settlement and the colonists were shipped back to France. Champlain was sent into **exile** in England.

(below) Champlain erected Habitation in Quebec City, Canada. The word Quebec means "the place where the river narrows" in the language of the Montagnais.

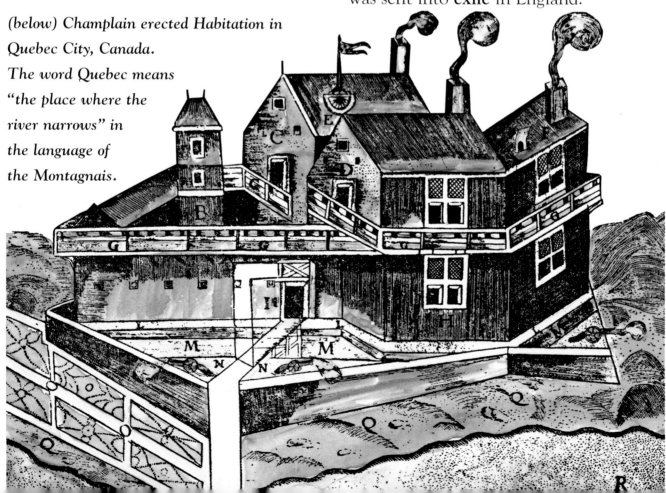

Reclaiming New France

While Champlain was in exile, England and France signed a **treaty** in which the English agreed to return control of New France to the French. Champlain returned from exile to France and left again for Habitation in 1632, but when he arrived he found that the English had left the settlement in ruins. The French worked to rebuild it and by 1634, new crops were growing, a church was built, and Habitation was flourishing.

(background) After an English blockade of supply ships nearly starved Habitation, Champlain surrendered to David Kirk in 1629.

Life in the Colony

Habitation had humble beginnings, but over time, it became a large, successful settlement with many colonists, houses, and churches. The dominant trades included farming, fishing, and fur trading.

The Homestead

Most homes in New France were built of wood because there were many trees available and it was a good insulator against the cold winters. The roofs were made of **thatch** or wooden boards, and were sloped so that the snow slid off. Most homesteads had vegetable gardens which included cabbage, cucumbers, and beans, and crops of wheat and rye were also grown. By 1700, many colonists in New France raised livestock, such as oxen, pigs, poultry, and cattle, for work and for food.

Pea Pottage

The colonists had supplies of fresh and dried peas and beans, corn, and animal fats. They used these to make a thick soup called pottage. Pottage might even have been served by the Order of Good Cheer. Ask an adult to help you cook a pot of pottage.

1 tbsp (15 mL) butter
1 medium onion, chopped
5 cups (1200 mL) frozen peas
3-4 cups (700 - 950 mL) chicken broth
Salt and pepper to taste
2/3 to 1 cup (157 - 237 mL) buttermilk

1. Heat the butter in a pot until melted.
2. Add onion and sauté for about five minutes or until softened.
3. Add the peas and broth and bring to a boil. Simmer, uncovered until the peas are tender.
4. Mash the soup by hand or purée in a blender. Add salt and pepper to taste and if needed, stir in the buttermilk.
Enjoy!

(below) The colonists adopted the Algonquian's birchbark canoes because they were lightweight and easy to maneuver. The delicate boats made it necessary for the colonists to carry supplies for repairs, such as extra birch bark, leather strips, and spruce or pine gum for waterproofing. Heavy goods were transported on large cedar rafts called cajeux.

Order of Good Cheer

While at Port Royal, Champlain established a club called The Order of Good Cheer to keep colonists in high spirits during the long winters. Each day, one man was named "Chief Steward and Caterer," and was required to prepare a special feast. The men competed to provide the most flavorful meal, and the menus included wild game such as bear, otter, beaver tails, and wildcat. When dinner was ready, the men paraded to the feast with the Steward leading, and they played music, danced, and sang songs.

Before Colonization

The Huron and Iroquois were at war before Champlain arrived in North America. The two groups were rivals for territory and trade in what is today upper New York State and southern Ontario.

The Huron, or Wendat

Huron is the French name for the Wendat, a group of four to six nations, or tribes, who lived in year-round permanent villages mostly in what is today southern Ontario. Although enemies with the Iroquois, the Huron belong to the Iroquoian family, a group of nations that have similar languages and lifestyles. The Huron peoples farmed, hunted, and traded. The French met the Huron in the early 1600s and became their trade allies. As allies, the French participated in Huron war raids on the Iroquois. These battles also made the French an enemy of the Iroquois and brought about a series of battles, **massacres**, and years of war.

(below) Many Native peoples, such as the Huron, grew and harvested crops, such as beans, squash, and maize, or corn.

(left) The Iroquois lived in longhouses that were about 200 feet (60 meters) long, framed with wood and covered with elm bark. Iroquois villages were large and fortified, and were moved when the soil became unable to support food crops.

The Iroquois

The Iroquois was a group of five different nations, called the Haudenosaunee Confederacy, or the Iroquois Confederacy. These nations, the Mohawk, Onondaga, Seneca, Cayuga, and Oneida, joined together many years before the arrival of Europeans, in an alliance for trade and to prevent war between them. The Confederacy's long-standing enemies were the Huron, Algonquin, and Montagnais. The Iroquois lived in the northeastern United States and eastern Canada. Iroquois women owned all property and tended crops of corn, squash, and beans. The men fished in spring and hunted in fall.

The Algonquin

The Algonquins, also known as the Algonkins, lived in villages in southern Quebec and eastern Ontario. They moved with the seasons to hunt and fish.

Algonquins returned to their villages in winter. When the French arrived, the Algonquin, like the Huron, were already warring with the Iroquois. They began a trading relationship and became allies of the French. The name Algonquian, with an "a" refers to a group of languages spoken by the Algonquin and many other Native nations in North America.

The Montagnais

The Montagnais, a French word for mountain people, lived in present-day Quebec and Labrador. They were a hunting and fishing people who today, along with the Naskapi people, are called the Innu. Montagnais land was not suitable for agriculture, so they hunted caribou and moose and fished for eel, fish, and seals. Montagnais homes were made of birch bark. The French traded with the Montagnais and became their allies in wars against the Iroquois.

Life After Champlain

Champlain dreamed that the furs and farmland of New France would one day make it strong, but the colony's future depended on the growth of its population. After Champlain's death, New France grew from hundreds of settlers to thousands.

What Happened to Champlain?

While at Habitation in 1635, Champlain suffered a stroke and was confined to his bed. When Champlain died, the French colonists mourned the loss of their leader. His Native allies gave the colonists furs to honor Champlain and he was buried beneath the floor of Notre Dame de la Recouvrance church. A chapel was built over his grave in his honor.

Relations with the Iroquois

After Champlain's death, the hostility between the French, their allies, and the Iroquois continued until the Huron were defeated in 1650. France's King Louis XIV took control of New France in 1663, and shipped 1,300 soldiers from France to defend it against the Iroquois. In July 1667, the Iroquois and the French signed a peace treaty.

(below) The French sent priests on fur trading missions to convert Native peoples to Christianity.

New France Settlements

France's King Louis XIV shipped more settlers to New France to increase the population of the settlements in present-day Quebec City, as well as Montreal, and Trois Rivieres. Many peasant farmers came from France for the farmland, the hunting, and the fishing. Between 1665 and 1671, more than 1,100 women immigrated to New France. The French government awarded money to the settlers for marrying and raising large families.

(above) The Iroquois traded pelts, especially beaver, to the Dutch who settled in present-day New York in return for firearms. The Iroquois used these guns to dominate fur trade routes and attack French and Huron settlements.

England's Victory

In 1670, England gave the Hudson's Bay Company control of the fur trade in all territories surrounding Hudson Bay. This meant less fur and profit for the French, who fought battles against the British, and gained control of many English forts. After a war in Europe in 1713, France was forced to give the British control over Hudson Bay, Newfoundland, and Acadia. In 1760, the British and French began a fierce battle for control of New France, ending with New France's surrender to England.

Champlain's Legacy

Samuel de Champlain is known today as an intrepid, or fearless, and determined explorer. He is also remembered as the founder of New France and a leader who asserted a French presence in North America.

French Influence

Champlain's early settlements in New France helped secure the presence of a French culture and language in North America. French is the main language in Quebec and New Brunswick, and is also spoken in other Canadian provinces. Habitation is now Quebec City, the capital of the Canadian province of Quebec. French fur traders explored the lakes and rivers of North America and French settlers worked the land. Many landmarks in North America were named by these traders, explorers, and settlers, including the cities of Detroit Michigan, Bayonne New Jersey, Au Claire, La Crosse, and Fond du Lac, Wisconsin, as well as the state of Vermont.

Native Lands

After Europeans arrived in North America, the lives of the Native peoples changed. Conflicts among Native groups increased when they allied with different European peoples in battles for control of the fur trade. Europeans took control of the Native peoples' lands and forced them to abandon their own spiritual beliefs and adopt Christianity. Many Native peoples died in battles and from European diseases. Today, Native peoples are reclaiming their heritage and lands.

(left) There are many monuments that honor Champlain throughout Canada and the United States. This statue of Champlain, in Ottawa, Ontario, overlooks the Ottawa River and the far bank of Hull, Quebec.

(background) Quebecers wave the blue and white Fleur-de-Lis flag of Quebec during Saint-Jean-Baptiste Day celebrations. The annual holiday was first celebrated as a religious event in 1615, but is now a provincial holiday in Quebec.

Glossary

alliance A partnership between peoples or countries

Arab A person from the Middle East or North Africa who speaks the Arabic language

arquebus A heavy, portable gun invented during the 1400s

barricade A structure built to block passage or attack

Christianity A religion based on the teachings of Jesus Christ, whom Christians believe is the son of God

colony Territory that is ruled by another country

commodity Something that is bought and sold

confession When someone admits to a crime or moral sin

convert To change from one religion or belief to another

dysentery A sickness that causes diarrhea

exile To force a person to leave his or her country or home

fertile Describing land that is able to produce abundant crops or vegetation

forge A place where metal is heated and hammered into useful objects, such as tools

fortify To make strong to defend against attack

Haudenosaunee A group of native North American peoples who banded together before European contact, in a confederation also called the Iroquois Confederacy

interpreter Someone who translates words from one language to another

mass A religious celebration in the Roman Catholic Church

massacre The brutal killing of large numbers of humans or animals

Middle Ages The period in European history from about 500 A.D. to about 1500

monopoly Control over a product or a service

navigate To direct the course, or direction, of a ship

nobility The most powerful or wealthy group in a society

rampart A wall or bank of earth raised around a structure for protection against attack

ration A set and usually small portion of a provision, such as food

Roman Catholic A Christian religion. The leader of the Roman Catholic Church is the pope

rye A grass or cereal crop used to make flour for bread

settlement A newly colonized, or settled in, region

stonemason A builder that works with stone

thatch Straw, reeds, or grass that is woven together and used as a roof

treaty An official agreement between two or more countries, governments, or rulers

Index

1 2 3 4 5 6 7 8 9 0 Printed in the U.S.A. 4 3 2 1 0 9 8 7 6 5
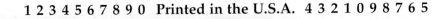